The Gates of Charleston

Photographs and Text

by

William Murry Thompson

The cooperation of Philip Simmons and the Philip Simmons Foundation, PO Box 21585, Charleston, S. C., 29413, are appreciated. The help of Anna Taylor Blythe whose local knowledge amassed through years of conducting walking tours of the city was invaluable and also appreciated. Judy Anneaux graciously provided editorial services.

FIRST EDITION

Published by W. Thompson
809 Burnett Drive, Charleston, S. C., 29412

To order additional copies, please contact us.
BookSurge, LLC
www.booksurge.com
1-866-308-6235
orders@booksurge.com

Preface

A gate is not simply a door to keep things out. It may be an invitation to enter, a thing of beauty in its self, a frame for a house and garden, a point of leaving and return, or a demarcation of where the home begins and the outside ends. As much as any other part of a home, it reflects the personality and style of the owner. The gates of Charleston together with the lovely historic homes and gardens behind them are the classic examples of the blending of these elements. No other city offers the visitor roaming the streets a more delightful panorama of vistas to wile away the hours. Whether viewing while walking, from a bicycle, a carriage or an auto, it is just one beautiful discovery after another. Early gates were imported from Europe together with settlers possessing iron-working skills. This was followed by the development of colonial artistry and forms. The altar rail of Saint Michael's was imported in 1772 and served as a model of advanced artistry for the local ironworkers. Early ironworkers included suppliers to the Continental Army such as Tunis Tebout and William Johnson. The historical background of the sites also adds interest. The beauty, artistry and appreciation of ironwork are such that several gates to nowhere have been erected. They are simply there to be admired as works of art. Such is the case at the Charleston Visitors Center, the Waterfront Park, the South Carolina State Museum, as well as the gazebo inside the terminal at the airport. Old gates are often retained with their pillars after the walls have been removed or kept closed after the gates are no longer required for access. The hidden location of many gates gives gate searching the nature of a treasure hunt.

Saint Michael's Altar Rail

10 Archdale Street

The Saint John's Lutheran Church was built 1815-1817. The gates were designed in 1822 by the church architect Abraham Reeves and made by J. F. Roh.

10 Archdale Street

The north gate is one of six gates to the church property and is seldom used. The design, though similar to that of the three sets at the front of the church, is considerably different in detail.

10 Archdale Street

Saint John's Lutheran Church

Ashley Hall Smith Street Gate

(172 Rutledge Ave.) The main building at Ashley Hall was the former residence of George Trenholm, the second Treasurer of the Confederacy. He was responsible for much of the blockade running, and is reputed to be the model for Rhett Butler.

ENTRANCE

Bethany Cemetery

The main gate on Cunnungton Street located off Meeting Street.

Bethany Cemetery

It is located with the major cemeteries north of the city. Within the cemetery main gates stands these gates to an internal plot.

67 Broad Street

The gate design is by R. M. Hollins and fabricated by Philip Simmons.

80 Broad Street

The Broad Street entrance gate to the Washington Square Park. This is one of five gates to the park, all built to a similar design. The old park was refurbished and named by the Washington Light Infantry in 1881.

116 Broad Street

The Rutledge House Inn was the former home of a wealthy slave trader, Thomas Norman Gadsden. The original house is pre-revolutionary and was remodeled in 1853. The ironwork added at that time is by Christopher Werner. The posts contain the Federal Eagle and the South Carolina Palmetto Tree. Dragons hold the rail on the balcony.

117 Broad Street, The Governor's House Inn

The house, c. 1760, was the home of Governor Edward Rutledge, the youngest signer of the Declaration of Independence.

121 Broad Street

Saint John the Baptist Office.

122 Broad Street

This simple gate leads to the grand Catholic Cathedral of Saint John The Baptist.

167 Broad Street

The Heilbron-Gibbon House. c. 1836-40. This home was one of the few west of Legare and on the south side of Broad to survive the fire of 1861.

167 Calhoun Street

The College of Charleston Calhoun Street entrance gates are designed by Albert Simons and built by McClammy Iron Works .

Chalmers Street, Washington Square,

This is one of the smaller gates to the park. It is said to be designed by Christopher Werner.

32 Chalmers St.

The houses in this area were demolished by the Citizens and Southern Bank to provide a parking lot. The new grounds from the 1960's are by Robert Martin of Walterboro who also designed the grounds for the headquarters of the Southern Living magazine.

38 Chalmers Street

This is an interesting gate because of the fixed spiked guard above the gate called Cha de Frise or Chevaux de Frise; Literally, "Horses of Friesland." Attacked by cavalry, the people of Friesland on the Baltic fortified their city with spikes to prevent horses from jumping over the walls and gates.

39 Church Street

The George Eveleigh House. 1743.

133 Church Street

Dock Street Theatre. 1835. Formerly the Planters Hotel These gates at the Dock Street Theater are from the 1935 restoration and are by Albert Simons, FAIA.

145 Church Street, Pirate's Courtyard

Located across the street from Saint Philip's Church, this was a gathering place for pirates. It is reputed that in this house Stede Bonnet hid his treasure. He was later captured and hanged at White Point Gardens (The Battery).

146 Church Street, Saint Philip's Church South Gate

The gates are thought to date from 1838 possibly designed by Joseph Hyde in 1836. He was the architect of the second church built here. The railings were originally around the City Hall. This gate leads to one of the more interesting cemeteries in Charleston where Edward Rutledge, a signer of the Declaration of Independence is buried.

146 Church Street, Saint Philip's Cemetery

This gate of the west cemetery, directly across the street from the church, leads to the grave of Vice President John C. Calhoun and DuBose Heyward who wrote the libretto of Porgy and Bess. The west gate is one of the only pre-Revolutionary gates in the city.

Citadel Main Gate

171 Moultrie Street, The Military College of South Carolina.

Citadel North Gate

These gates in the style of the sword gates were later additions. The lighter gauge ironwork has been bent by people who apparently use the gate as a ladder.

126 Coming Street

The Cathedral of Saint Luke and Saint Paul dates to 1816. The original planned steeple was omitted when settling and cracking in the walls were encountered during construction. Modification work continues still. The gate is almost identical to the 53 Meeting Street gate at the First Scots Presbyterian Church built in 1814.

21 East Bay

Edmondston-Alston House This house is a house museum of the Middleton Place Foundation. It was built in 1825 by Charles Edmondston and sold in 1838 to Charles Alston. In 1861 the Alston family and General P. G. T. Beauregard viewed the bombardment of Fort Sumter from the piazzas of this house.

51 East Bay

The Casper Christian Schutt house was built in 1800-1802 as one of the largest homes in Charleston. Its three piazzas with Doric, Ionic and Corinthian columns in ascending order are unique. These gates are from a 1994-95 restoration. It remains a single family residence.

329 East Bay Street

The Gadsen-Morris House. c. 1800. This gate from about 1960 was designed by S. G. Stoney and crafted by Philip Simmons. The snake probably represents the "Don't tread on me" flag of the 1775 Continental Navy.

332 East Bay Street

The Robert Pimrose House. c.1817. The gates date from the mid-1800s.

66 George Street, East Gate

The College of Charleston, c 1820-56. The center of the campus is around a cistern before the main building; The Harrison-Randolph Hall. c. 1828. This area is bounded by George Street, Green Street, Coming Street and Saint Philip Street and includes several gates. The wrought-iron fence around the area is by Christopher Werner, who also probably provided the gates around 1852 including those of the Old Porters Lodge.

66 George Street

College of Charleston Kathleen Lightly Garden. Located to the east of the main building is this delightful gate to a small garden.

11 George Street

The Old Porters Lodge gates on the south side of the cistern campus are by C. Werner from around 1852.

ΓΝΩΘΙ ΣΑΥΤΟΝ

66 George Street

The College of Charleston campus west gate was erected in 1929 to commemorate the establishment of the Pi Kappa Phi fraternity here in 1908.

George Alfred Trenholm

George Alfred Trenholm is a Charlestonian whose name is often seen in this book but may not be widely known as he was not a military man or a prominent politician. He was in the shipping business and played a large part in the blockade running of the Civil War. As Secretary of Treasury of the Confederacy the last year of the war, his company controlled some sixty blockade-running ships. He became the richest man in the South and held vast property interests. He owned several homes in Charleston including Ashley Hall, the Planters Hotel that is the Dock Street Theater, a house in Richmond, plantations and commercial buildings. He was prominent in the church and the establishment of hospitals, schools and orphanages. At the end of the war as Richmond was falling, the assets of the treasury were shipped to Charleston. While the silver was accounted for, the gold vanished. Trenholm was indicted and jailed possibly in an attempt of extortion. His property was seized by the Federal government, but he was soon released. He received a pardon from President Andrew Johnston. The gold and other treasures were never recovered. The question of whom owed what to whom was complicated at the time.

Trenholm died in 1876, days after the "carpet bag governor" was removed from the State House. Metal detectors have been frequently swung and privies around his properties dug up for years with no known discoveries to date. He was related to Margaret Mitchell and widely considered to be the model for her Rhett Butler in her "Gone With the Wind."

George Alfred Trenholm

14 Green Street

Knox-Lesene House. c. 1846. One block south of Calhoun Street is Green Street. Only one block long, it is swallowed in the College of Charleston campus. With a brick side-walk and landscaping, the street no longer exists, but the beautiful old homes and this gate in particular still stand. It was the home of African-American Albert Osceola Jones who was state representative 1870-1881.

6 Gibbs Street

Parker-DraytonHouse. c. 1806. The windows of this house once overlooked the Ashley River.

64

64 Hasell Street

The Benjamin Smith House. c. 1843. The single gate probably dates from the original house.

95 Hasell Street

St. Mary's Roman Catholic Church dates from 1789 when the site was first used for worship. This structure was built in 1839. It is the mother church for Carolina and Georgia.The gates are from the original building.

Huguenin Avenue
Magnolia Cemetery

This cemetery is the burial site of many Charlestonian notables. A stone with only his birth and death dates and initials mark the grave of George Trenholm. The crew of the Hunley is also buried here.

Huguenin Avenue
Saint Lawrence Catholic Cemetery

This gate is located to the right of the Magnolia Cemetery.

Philip Simmons

Philip Simmons is a name that is synonymous with Charleston gates. This blacksmith is renowned for his artistry and workmanship. Born in 1912 on Daniel Island, he learned the smith work from Peter Simmons born in 1855. From the age of thirteen he was working with blacksmithing in the area at the east end of Calhoun Street where his shop is still located on Blake Street. In addition to the numerous gates and other ironwork in Charleston, he has been commissioned for work throughout the area. A double gate by him is in the South Carolina State Museum, and the centerpiece of the Charleston Airport is one of his large cupolas incorporating seating. His work is identified where shown. There is a Philip Simmons Garden behind the church just east of the Gaillard Auditorium. The Philip Simmons Foundation Inc. can be contacted at P. O. Box 21585, Charleston, SC, 29413-1585. The foundation administrator, Rossie M. Colter, was particularly helpful with the identification of Philip Simmons works in the area.

Philip Simmons and the author on Mr. Simmon's front porch.

5 King Street

21 King Street

The Patrick O'Donnell House was built 1852-1870. Author Josephine Pinckney who lived here 1907-39 was instrumental in the formation of the Poetry Society. The gates are from the 1980-1990s period.

27 King Street

The Miles Brewton House. c. 1769. In 1865 this was the Federal Headquarters for Generals Mead and Hatch. The gates and fence are pre-Revolutionary. The Cha de Fries were added after 1822. The gate overthrow contains a baroque shell.

82 King Street

The Robert Haig House. c. 1786. The porch was added in 1815 with further restorations made in the 1930s and 1990.

163 King Street

This Gateway Walk King Street gate is opposite the Charleston Library Society. It is from about 1930 by the Ortmann Brothers.

164 King Street

This is a Gateway Walk gate between the Charleston Library Society and the Charleston Art Museum. It is the original 1840 gate by C. Werner from the railroad office at 446 King Street. It was relocated here in 1930.

456 King Street

The William Aiken House was built in 1811. It was the home of Aiken, the President of the S. C. Canal and Railroad Company which was founded in 1830. This was the longest railroad in the U. S. and the first railroad to carry mail. After the offices here closed, the original gates and fence were moved in 1930 to the Gateway Walk between Archdale Street and Philadelphia Alley. When the house was restored in 2002, Philip Rogers imported identical metric iron stock from Europe to replicate the gates.

8 Legare Street

The drive gate is unique in that it contains a smaller wicket gate. The panel on the right can be opened independently from the main gate, The gate by C. W. Ortmann dates to 1901.

8 Legare Street

The main entrance gate is an older lyre design by C. Werner and thought to be original to the 1858 house

10

10 Legare Street

This gate of wrought iron and is from before 1861.

14 Legare Street

The Simmons-Edwards House was built by Francis Simmons in 1800. The gates, built from castings, are from before 1861. He reportedly left his new wife on Tradd Street to live in this house here. A friendly relationship existed thereafter. The finials were ordered from Italy to be in the form of acorns. They were rendered more in a pineapple-pine cone shape.The overall design from 1816 is by George Edwards.

26 Legare Street

The Whaley House

32 Legare Street

This is the location of the original Soloman Legare house. The sword gate was one of a set of two by Christopher Werner who came to Charleston in 1828. The two sets were made in 1838 for a city guardhouse. The gates used, were later moved to the Citadel on either side the main gate. The second set was bought by Mr. Hopley and placed here. Madam Talvande ran a boarding school for girls here. The high wall was reportedly built after one of the girls eloped from the school.

2 Meeting Street

Two Meeting Street Inn was built in 1892. The Tiffany windows in the house are reputed to have been built and installed by Tiffany himself.

.

15 Meeting Street

John Edwards House. c. 1770.

2

21 Meeting Street

27 Meeting Street

One of three houses (23, 25 and 27) built 1750-1790. The very detailed cast ironwork is from the Savannah Ironworks. The single homes are much alike, but yet, differ in variations.

32 Meeting Street

34 Meeting Street

Built around 1759, this was the home of Lord William Campbell, the last royal governor of South Carolina. Known as the Daniel E. Huger house, it was damaged during the shelling from 1863 to 1865 and subsequently looted by Union troops. These gates are by Philip Simmons. The house was last sold in 1819. The garden is by Loutrell Briggs.

36 Meeting Street

This house was built in 1740. The gates are by Philip Simmons who found a panel from a Broad Street bank on a trash pile and replicated it for two of the three panels.

37 Meeting Streeet

Otis Mills purchased this house in 1846. It was later the residence of General Beauregard. The gates and railings are thought to be from the mid-19th century remodeling of this 1778 house.

43 Meeting Street

James Mitchell House. c. 1798. The gates and ironwork were locally made in 1940s by the Sabel Ironworks. Owned now by Elizabeth Young, the property boasts beautiful gardens going back to Price's Alley.

45 Meeting Street

The gate and balustrade were crafted by Philip Simmons.

45

47 Meeting Street

The house is owned by Martha Rivers Ingram, Tennessee's only billionaire. The garden is by Robert Chestnut.

51 Meeting Street

The Nathaniel Russell house was built in 1808. The white ironwork was returned to its original color during a 1998 refurbishment by Berry Bates, a woman blacksmith who is the Artistic Director of The Asheville Ironworks. The fence came from the Radcliffe-Kiry house on George and Meeting Streets, the old College of Charleston gym site.

56 Meeting Street

The gate and railing were from the G, Manigault house on the southeast corner of Meeting and George streets. It was destroyed in 1930.

80 Meeting Street, Saint Michael's East Cemetery Gate Facing Broad Street

80 Meeting Street, Saint Michael's Cemetery Gate

This is the oldest church in the city and built in 1752-61. General Robert E. Lee worshiped here in 1861 in pew 43. Member Theodore Wagner offered bounties for the sinking of blockading ships. His brother, Col. Thomas Wagner served as Commander of Fort Sumter and constructed Battery Gregg on Morris Island. Battery Wagner, the site of the battle in the film "Glory," was named after him. He is buried in the churchyard. Two signers of the U. S. Constitution are buried here. These gates are from 1840 by the German ironworker J. A. W. Iusti. These gates facing Meeting Street and the east gates just behind the church facing Broad Street are identical. The unique lighting in the picture of the east gate on the preceding page shows better the intricate detail.

Located above the gate is an identifying plate of the manufacturer. It is badly corroded with the name Iusti barely visible.

Manufacturer identification plate above the gate

HOURS
Sunday
Tuesday
Thursday
Weekdays

90 Meeting Street

This is one of three sets of double gates at Washington Square. They are by C. Werner from about 1858.

105 Meeting Street

The Hibernian Society Hall, home to the Irish fraternal organization Ancient Order Hibernians, was established in 1801. The structure was built in 1840.

VALOR AND VIRTUE
WASHINGTON
1812
1836
1847
1861
1917
1941
THE SOUTH CAROLINA
SEA GRANT CONSORTIUM
SEA GRANT COLLEGE
WASHINGTON LIGHT INFANTRY

287 Meeting Street

Der Deutsche Freundndschaftsbund Hall. c. 1870. The Sea Grant College is dedicated to the wise use of marine resources. The gate was designed earlier by Albert Simons. The seal above the gate is that of the Washington Light Infantry founded in 1807 and active in every war since. The dates are those of the battles and the victories won since inception of the Washington Light Infantry. Their seal with the winged victory flying through the clouds lauds valor and the goddess Victory.

375 Meeting Street

Carolina Railroad Depot. c. 1850. 1870. These Peacock gate to nowhere are by Philip Simmons. They are found at the Charleston Visitor's Center at the old Charleston Railroad Depot. This was a hub of activity during the Civil War. Jefferson Davis arrived here in 1863, and the Ann Street depot was used as a hospital that was founded by George Trenholm.

Menotti Street

Across the street from the auditorium, behind the church is the Philip Simmons Garden. This double heart gate is at the entrance.

Old City Jail

The property at Franklin and Magazine Streets was designated public land in 1680. It was the site of the lunatic asylum, public burying grounds, poorhouse, powder magazines, hospitals, slave workhouse and the jail. The jail, c. 1802, held soldiers from the Mass. 54th volunteers captured from the action at Battery Wagner as was shown in the movie "Glory." Later, George Trenholm, the second Secretary of the Treasury for the Confederacy, was jailed here for suspected treason, possibly in connection with lost treasure from the shipments of funds from Richmond at the close of the war.

172 Rutledge Avenue

This is an internal gate that remains from earlier buildings on the Ashley Hall Campus.

182 Rutledge Avenue

The Beth Shalom Israel Temple was built in 1945. The Shalom group merged in 1955. The gates appropriately incorporate the Jewish elements.

2 Saint Michael's Alley

This beautiful gate is difficult to find. It is in the back of the garage and may be behind a parked car. This small gate made by Philip Simmons is one of his most beautiful. It was designed by the Reverend William Rhett.

134 Saint Philip Street

Saint Patrick's Roman Catholic Church.

55 Society Street

The High School of Charleston. c. 1840. The portico was added in 1850. Matching gates were placed on both sides of the porch, similar to gates of the 1840 period and were probably installed at that time.

32 South Battery

The Col. John Ashe House. c. 1782. Note that the carriage gate has a smaller wicket gate built into the left side of the main gate.

58 South Battery

The John Blake house was built in 1798. He was a Captain in the Continental Army and President of the Bank of South Carolina. This house originally overlooked the Ashley River. The gardens are by Lontrell Briggs.

68 South Battery

The Harth-Middleton House built in 1797. A house restoration was completed in 1920, and a garden by Loutrel Briggs was added to the west.

68 South Battery

The Harth-Middlton House garden gates and fence were relocated from 96 Rutledge Avenue. The Spoleto's logo was inspired by the circular elements of this gate.

68 South Battery

The house was built by John Harth in 1797. It was later sold to Henry Augustus Middleton. The balcony is from 87 East Bay Street.

5 Stoll's Alley

These were the first gates made by Philip Simmons around 1939.

9 Stoll's Alley

This gate is an early Philip Simmons work from 1939. Several of his early gates are found in this alley.

6 Thomas Street

The Legare-Rhett House. c. 1853. This is the Vanderhorst Street gate. This was the pre-Civil War home of Robert Barnwell Rett who owned the Charleston newspaper, The Charleston Mercury. The house was sold to Robert Trenholm. It is said that a soldier bode farewell to his love at this gate. She promised that the gate would remain locked until his return. The gate remains locked. The Hanckel family held the property for seventy-five years.

6 Tradd Street

The Allen-Hext Tenements at 5-7 Tradd Street were originally built in 1727 and have been rebuilt several times since. In 1785, No. 7 served as a grocery store.

100 Tradd Street

The house was built in 1790 for Capt. Francis Baker. The gate is by Philip Simmons.

122 Tradd Street

The William C. Bee House. c. 1850. This carriage gate has a wicket in the right side. Bee was a leading blockade runner during the Civil War and also helped establish the phosphate business in Charleston.

143 Tradd Street

The Bowles-Legare-Parker House. c. 1797-1801. Solomon Legare Jr. remodeled the home. The gates of wrought and cast iron are combined in a crossed arrow design.

Waterfront Park

These gates are welded open making it difficult to see the beautiful egrets in each. They are by Philip Simmons.

23 Wentworth Street

The James J. Jeffords House. c. 1843. The gates were probably added as a part of a 1966 restoration.

43 Wentworth Street

The Saint Andrew's Lutheran Church. c. 1840. There have been several subsequent alterations. The gates are later additions by Philip Simmons.

60 Wentworth Street

Centenary United Methodist Church. c. 1841.

138 Wentworth Street

The Edwin L. Kerrison House. c. 1838. Built by a dry goods merchant, the house was restored in the 1970s. These gates are by Philip Simmons. It was previously the Episcopal Diocesan Office.

149 Wentworth Street

Francis Silas Rodgers Mansion. Constructed 1885-87. The Wentworth Mansion has both notable gate and banister rails. It was the home of Fire Marshal Francis Silas Rodgers whose family held it until 1920. Currently it is an inn with The Circa 1886 Restaurant in the back area.

In Conclusion

So, these are the gates of Charleston, not all the gates, but most of the more fascinating and sufficient to provide a good taste of what is here and inspire a further independent exploration of your own. Over the past four hundred years, the function of the gate has changed somewhat from that of protection to that of the confinement of children and pets. This usage is mixed with an increasing appreciation as a work of art as evidenced by the private and public underwriting of non-functioning new gates and preservation of those historical. The story of a gate from the physical properties, the ironwork technology, techniques, the artist designer and builder, the grounds and buildings, the property owners and the surrounding stream of personalities and history could result in a book on each gate. Accordingly, the descriptions have been reduced to the minimum to present the gates without distraction. The information has been gleaned to avoid repetition and incidental detail. The photographic beauty of each gate is the best description to be offered. Hopefully, the reader's interest will be motivated to pursue those stories and further detail independently. If that is done, the purpose of the book has been well served. Gaze at these works of art. As you stroll the streets, free your imagination to wander through the centuries of history. Place yourself in the Charleston of that era and enjoy. For those notable gates which have been omitted, there is left all the more for your discovery.

Bibliography

Bayliss, Charles N., Charleston Ironwork, Pennsylvania, 2002

Bragg, Laura M., Manuscript in S. C. Historical Society, Charleston, S. C., c. 1925.

Coy, Mary Clark, The Civil War Walking History Book, Charleston, S. C., 1999

Nepveux, Ethel Trenholm Seabrook, George Alfred Trenholm, The Company That Went to War 1861-1865, Charleston, S. C., 1973.

Poston, Jonathan H., The Buildings of Charleston, Columbia, S. C., 1997.

Spence, E. Lee, Treasures of the Confederate Coast, The Real Rhett Butler and Other Revelations, Miami FL/Charleston SC, 1995

Swann, Nita, The Complete Walking Tour of Historic Charleston, Charleston, S. C., 1986

Thompson, Joseph F., The Doors and Gates Of Charleston, Columbia, S. C., 1991

Vlach, John Michael, Charleston Blacksmith, The Work of Philip Simmons, Georgia and S. C., 1981, 1992